FINDING YOUR NEW NORMAL

GROWING FROM GRIEF TO GRACE

SHANNON DAVIS-WILLS, MA

CONTENTS

All Scripture quotations, unless otherwise indicated, are from the Holy Bible, New King James Version, copyrighted 1979, 1980, 1982, 1991 by Thomas Nelson, Inc.

ISBN: 9781798069554

❀ Created with Vellum

~

This book is lovingly dedicated to my parents, Donald and Deborah. Without these two beautiful souls, I would not be here. Dad didn't tell me how to live my life, but he showed me how to. He taught me how to live by my own set of rules and celebrate every day. Mom not only showed me how to be a strong African American woman, she also modeled unconditional love even when it was tough. She taught me no matter the obstacle, I can always overcome and recover. I am eternally grateful for their love and support.

In Loving Memory of
André, Sr.
Micheal Robertson
Nathaniel Robertson
June "Cookie" Williams

ACKNOWLEDGMENTS

The process of writing a book takes much detail and planning. However, my conviction that this book needed to be written was unwavering. I could not have done it alone. Many people helped shape and mold me into the person I am today. I want to thank each of you for the experience and life lessons. Many people have also inspired, motivated, and prayed to bring this book to fruition. I want to take a moment to thank them.

I cannot say enough about my mom and dad, Deborah and Donald. They exemplified unconditional love, even and especially when it was hard. They have always sustained me when they didn't understand or agree. I must acknowledge my dad for challenging me to read books that embraced our cultural diversity and struggles as African Americans, thus sparking my interest and love of reading.

I have to thank my mom for making sure education was a priority. She maintained an extensive library that expanded my imagination and satisfied my thirst for knowledge at the same time. Both of my parents have stood by me and because of them, I have the courage to share my story.

Michael, my love, I have to give thanks for your support in allowing me to continue to heal in His presence. Words cannot express what your love and comfort mean to me. You love me with my flaws and all. Thanks for allowing me to express my feelings and embracing the person I am becoming. I am grateful you are a part of this journey.

My inspiration and motivation come from my children, Joshua, Jacob, Yasmin, Desmond, and my bonus children, Jhaylia and Andre, Jr. Everything I do is with them in mind. I want to be a role-model and demonstrate you can conquer anything in your path. I pray they continue to put God first and understand nothing comes without hard work and sacrifice.

I have to recognize my prayer warrior, Shantel. I called and challenged her with the task of continual prayer throughout the process of writing this book. She obliged and encouraged me to write this book and go beyond what I had planned. She inspired and pushed me to continue to walk in my purpose. Shantel had faith that I could finish this book and more when I doubted myself. She is not only my friend; she is my motivator and spiritual advisor.

Sometimes, we encounter individuals who inspire us by simply following God's calling for their life. I owe gratitude to Romella Vaughn. She did not hesitate in directing me on the right path to make sure this book came to fruition. She is truly a great mentor.

April Dishon Barker provided the developmental and contextual editing of this book. She has provided me guidance, direction, and support. Without her numerous phone calls and texts to keep me focused and on task, I would not have completed this book. She stayed the course with me and made sure I stayed on course as well. I will forever be indebted to her.

The staff at EBM Professional Services was remarkable. Thanks goes to Michelle. Her contributions enhanced this project. Her professionalism and timely feedback were impeccable.

Grant Partners Gospel provided the amazing artwork for the cover of this book. I have worked with Derrick on other projects. He has the gift of putting your words into art. I am truly grateful.

I cannot express the gratitude I have for my extended family and close friends. The last ten years has been a growing process for me. They stood beside me even when they didn't understand me. This book would not be possible without their unyielding support and love. If I have not mentioned you by name, please know I am grateful for any deed that went forth in helping with the completion of this book.

Last, but definitely not least, I have to thank God. He ushered me into this journey and kept me through it. The conviction to write this book was given to me years ago and God never let me forget His will for me. I can truly say this book was inspired by God.

INTRODUCTION

"Weeping may endure for a night,
But joy comes in the morning."
Psalm 30:5 NKJV

This transformational expedition begun in 2008. My husband died un-expectantly that year. My life as I knew it was forever changed. I was forced into a position I was not prepared for. Well, I thought I wasn't ready. As I reflect on my journey, I realized God was teaching and equipping me with the tools I needed all along.

How to cry when no one is looking are the words

God whispered to me one day. I can remember that day like it was yesterday. It was a few years after my husband died. I was on Cockrell Hill Street driving home from class. Those words echoed over and over until I realized God had given me the title to a book. I know without a doubt God wanted me to help others who had experienced the same type of loss I did. What I didn't know is that He wanted me to write a book. The notion appeared silly and unreal at first. I am not an author and writing is not my favorite subject or strong suit. I tried to ignore God's calling. I thought, surely, someone else was well equipped and more knowledgeable than me to complete the task at hand. The thought of writing a book continued to invade my mind. Months would go by and I would not entertain the notion of writing a book, then the idea would flood my mind again. I could not shake it.

One particular Sunday, I had a hard time getting out of bed to go to church. My alarm sounded, but I went back to sleep. I had no intentions on going to church that Sunday. God had other plans for me. I woke back up an hour later, got dressed, and planned to attend church service alone. I prayed in the car on my way to church. I asked God for forgiveness because this wasn't the first time I turned the alarm off and went back to sleep. It was becoming a habit I needed to break. My pastor spoke about unfulfilled dreams and reoccurring thoughts. He explained, the reason the thought would not go away is because God is calling you to finish a mission. God planted the idea and expects us to follow through. I needed to hear that. God would not allow me to sleep through that message because it's what motivated me to start the task of writing this book. I left church feeling revived and refreshed. I thought, *That sermon was for me.* Now, it's time for me to get started.

I didn't set out to write a book just to share my testimony. I wanted to give people something they can utilize in their daily walk with Christ. It's easy to praise and worship when things are good and you're surrounded by loved ones. However, I experienced first-hand the difficulty of getting out of bed and having no desire to attend church or any other place because I was in so much pain. I understand not wanting to go to church because the experience reminded me of the person who died. I can identify with how it feels to drive somewhere and not know how I got there. Then, completely break down in tears because I didn't have the strength to do anything else.

You have the urge to call a friend because you want to hear, "It's going to get better." You dial the number, but, change your mind because you realize he/she do not understand your pain and wouldn't know what to say. Finally, you conclude you really don't feel like burdening anyone with your emotional state. It's difficult getting past the pain and seeing beyond what is right now.

God whispered, *How to cry when no one is looking* to me because that's what my life reflected at the time. I was good at crying behind closed doors. I was great at presenting myself as a strong African American woman. I put on this tough front for everyone. I wanted to be strong for my children. I pretended to have everything in order. Friends and family often commented how they would not be able to move on after the loss of a spouse. Some would exclaim, "I don't know how you're doing it!" That was just it, I was just doing what I thought was needed to take care of my family.

The more the phrase: *how to cry when no one is looking* replayed in my mind, the more I reflected on my journey. I understood the calling to write a book. But I wasn't interested in writing a self-help book on masking pain. It didn't help me, and I'm pretty sure no one needs a manual on hiding emotions. I prayed that God would give me what's needed to help others and myself in the process.

Finding Your New Normal, as you know by now, was not the original title of this book. The phrase is dated, but still a popular and relevant one. I do not remember when I initially thought of it as a book title. I just know God inspired me. The day I claimed it as the title of this book, it truly resonated with me. I began to understand what it meant to me. I had to accept the fact that relationships and experiences would not be the same anymore.

I processed what my new normal looked like. I can tell you, honestly, I did not want to accept it because for years I would compare present relationships and experiences to my past. I was not willing or ready to let go. I longed to have my old life back. I missed the old me. I realized I was anguished over a life I could never have back.

I loved my husband deeply. I missed him immensely. I still think of him and the life we created. He will always be a part of my life. But, I recognized I was no longer mourning the death of my husband, I was grieving the safety and security I had. I was safe in knowing my late husband would take care of the family. We were always his number one priority. My late husband provided financial security. He supported my decision to go back to cosmetology school. He was willing to work two jobs so that I didn't have to work one.

Now, I had to provide for our children and myself. I had to create a safe environment for our children. Although, I didn't realize it until I was in the midst of redefining myself, I was finding my own new normal. This book is my journey of growing from grief to grace and to who I am now.

Finding your new normal is a progression. The process is about accepting what is new and letting go of what is old. It's not about getting over a tragedy or loss but moving and living through it. The process does not happen overnight. You cannot blink your eyes or wave a magic wand to whisk your pain away. Healing comes over time. After reading this book, I want you to know it's okay to take one day at a time. It's okay to allow yourself to feel. It's okay to redefine yourself. It's okay to move forward and begin again. Some days you will still cry and some days you will continue to laugh. Just remember, it's all a part of the healing process.

Dear Heavenly Father,

I pray whomever is reading this book gets what's needed to move forward with peace and healing.

In Your Son Jesus Name, Amen

HOW DID I GET HERE?

> *"A good name is better than*
> *precious ointment, And the day*
> *of death than the day of one's*
> *birth."*
> *Ecclesiastes 7:1 NKJV*

I was exposed to loss at an early age. Like many other children, I knew about death, but did not fully comprehend what it meant, how to grieve, or how to handle loss. My paternal grandmother and cousin died during my preteen years. I remember I did not wish to attend my cousin's funeral because I knew it would be sad.

My dad was furious at me and tried to explain the importance of paying my respects and attending the funeral. At the time, the explanation didn't register or makes sense to me. I just didn't want to be around sad people. It wasn't until I lost someone very close to me that I had a glimpse of the emotional toll grief has on the body and mind.

My uncle, Michael, was five years older than me. He was more like an older brother than an uncle because of our ages and family closeness. Michael loved to joke around. My aunt had recently recovered from chicken pox and she still had scars on her legs. I can recall one day Michael held up a chocolate chip cookie in the air and asked, "What does this remind y'all of?" Everyone looked at each other bewildered because we didn't have a clue. He then put the cookie next to my aunt's leg and we all burst into laughter. Now, her skin reflected that of a chocolate chip cookie because of the scars. He was the jokester of the family.

Michael's nickname for me was "Too Tall." It was after the NFL player, Ed "Too Tall" Jones because I was quite tall for my age. I can hear his voice now, "What's up, Too Tall?" I would just smile and laugh.

Michael was shot in the shoulder one day

during the summer. He was nineteen years old. It was the day before my cheerleading showcase. I had prepared and attended a cheerleading workshop all summer. The finale was the following day. Needless to say, I was never able to showcase my cheerleading talent or participate in cheerleading again. The gunshot wound did not kill Michael immediately, but it led to his death several months later. He had difficulty breathing after the gunshot wound and a tracheostomy was performed.

Eventually, Michael learned to talk with the trach tube and begin physical therapy. My family and I traveled back and forth to the hospital, then after some time passed to the rehab facility to visit my uncle over the course of seven months. He would always cry at the end of the visit, asking to go home with us. I could tell it tore my mom to pieces seeing him cry. It was always a quiet ride home.

One day, Michael's wish was granted and the doctor's allowed him a two day pass home. The family gathered and had a huge celebration. It was the first time in months we gathered together, laughed, and enjoyed each other's company. Michael was so excited to be home. He didn't want to return to the rehab facility. The decision was made to let him stay home an extra day. That extra day proved to be fatal. I'm still not sure what happened, but I know he returned to the rehab facility on a Sunday. Monday, Michael was placed on a ventilator and considered brain dead. The night he was taken off the ventilator, my mom asked if I wanted to go to the hospital. I declined and stayed at my grandmother's house with other family members. We didn't have another conversation afterwards in regard to my uncle's death.

The days leading up to Michael's funeral were sad. I witnessed my mother and grandmother plan his funeral. However, I do not remember them shedding tears. Of course, I didn't cry either because I'm witnessing these two strong, African American women hold it together. I thought I had to keep it composed as well.

I sat in his funeral listening to the pastor. I watched friends and family cry and comfort each other. I observed people view his body. Then, it was my turn to view my uncle's body. I stood up and walked to his casket. I looked at my uncle in the coffin, and the first thing I noticed was that he had a fresh haircut. I thought, *He doesn't look the same,* and proceeded back to my seat. On the way back to my seat, I realized I would never see my uncle again. I looked at my friend, who was standing behind me, and whispered, "I'm never going to see him again." All those tears I was holding back came pouring down. It was the realization that I would never have those brotherly moments again that bought me to tears.

I returned to school a few days later. I don't recall telling my friends my uncle died. It was as if I picked up where I left off at school. I played in the concert and marching band. However, I wasn't able to participate in some events because we were traveling to the hospital to visit my uncle. Now that I was back in school, I was able to be an active member of the band again. I witnessed my family continue their life, and I did as well, although I persistently wrestled with the fact I would not see my uncle again. This is how I learned to grieve.

It's important for me to share my experience with my uncle's death because this set the tone on how I was to handle grief and loss. Sometimes, adults do not realize the impact they have on children looking up to them. I only mimicked what my mom and grandmother modeled. Later, I would follow the same pattern. They were demonstrating how to be strong by not crying in front of me. My mom wanted to protect me and not share certain details. She didn't want me to be sad, therefore, she didn't bring up his death and tried to carry on as if nothing tragic happened. In hindsight, they were teaching me how to cry when no one was looking.

The death of my uncle was definitely life changing. However, his departure from this earth still did not prepare me for future loss. As a teenager, my body and mind were in the beginning phase of developing me into the person I am now. My thought process was different. I only thought of the moment. I was selfish. I was not focused on the future. I had no clue of what to expect from the world. My feminism and blackness were not fully evolved. Frankly, I'm not sure if I was introduced or understood the terms. The lens I viewed the world through was different. My worldview was being shaped by the events that were taking place.

As a mature women, I now understand that the experiences we sustain from birth to adolescence help us transition to adulthood. Our bodies develop during our teenage years, boys and men begin to notice us. Our clothes start to fit differently, and we learn what to wear to accent our body shape. This molds our self-consciousness because we become aware of what others think of us. This awareness shapes our thinking process because we start to incorporate how others feel in our decision making. People disappoint us and we begin to slowly build a wall around our hearts without consciously knowing it. It's an ongoing learning process.

Needless to say, the way I handle death and loss as an adult is much different than when I was a teenager. Death of a loved one brings about reflection. I always analyze my friendships and the people in my life after someone I know dies. I explore the what-ifs of life. I survey my relationship with Christ. I ask myself, *Am I doing what God requires of me? Am I fulfilling my purpose on this earth?* I question myself, my purpose, and my destination. It's a weeding phase for me. I begin to remove excess people and things. I pray for strength and perseverance during this phase.

With each loss, I begin to understand more and more that life is short and not to take it for granted. I formed relationships with others as an adult and begin to rely on them. A bond is much deeper as an adult because you have years invested with this person and share experiences. Death is not only about not seeing that person again, it's about losing a relationship. Sometimes, it's about losing a piece of yourself and not knowing how to heal. I would have to agree with Benjamin Franklin who once wisely stated, "In this world nothing can be said to be certain, except death and taxes. There is no escape. Knowing this still does not prepare me for the losses that lie ahead."

DEAR HEAVENLY FATHER,

I pray we release the bondage that is keeping us from moving forward.

In Your Son Jesus Name, Amen

HOW TO CRY WHEN NO ONE IS LOOKING

"For to me, to live is Christ, and to
die is gain. But if I live in the
flesh, this will mean fruit from
my labor; yet what I shall
choose I cannot tell. For I am
hard-pressed between the two,
having a desire to depart and be
with Christ, which is far
better."
Philippians1:21-23 NKJV

B y 2008, I had matured into this beautiful and head-strong African American female. I was intrigued by feminism and what it meant to go from being Black to African American. I traveled and met others from around the world. I lived in three different states and immersed myself in each culture. My experiences taught me that I can adapt and adjust. My New Orleans accent faded slowly. I had a near death experience that forced me to reflect on my journey and purpose. This led me to want to do more for other young females. I didn't want them to travel the same road I did to get to this point in my life.

Yes, my life was filled with hurt, loss, and disappointment. However, I was able to rebound and recover. I was happily married with three kids. We'd purchased our first home a few years earlier. My family was active members in church.

I had friends; however, we treated each other like family. We supported each other and held one another accountable. I was settled and comfortable with the way things were going for me and my family. I had just completed and graduated from cosmetology school, for the second time. I was now a licensed cosmetologist and awaited this new journey that laid ahead.

I applied and was accepted into Bible College. I wanted to mentor young women from a biblical perspective. I couldn't complain if I wanted to— 2008 was looking good so far. All those character-building obstacles I faced early in life were paying off. Things were finally going well, and I was happy and content.

As you know, some things do not go according to plan. My plans were altered the night before my birthday. It was a Tuesday night and I was cooking tacos, hence "Taco Tuesday". My husband was showing the boys how to sort laundry. Afterwards, he headed back to the living room to watch a movie. My husband fainted in our living room while I was in the kitchen cooking. I called the paramedics and then my mom. She arrived before the paramedics did. When the paramedics reached our home, they were able to revive him, however, they brought him to the hospital for precaution. I called my friend, Shantel, on the way to the hospital and explained the events that just took place. She made it there before I did.

I arrived at the hospital and a doctor ushered us

into this room. By this time, my pastor, friends, and Uncle Raymond were all at the hospital as well. The hospital chaplain and doctor explained my husband developed an embolism that traveled to his lungs. This was the reason he fainted. The doctor continued to say they would do a procedure to prevent another blood clot from developing and if he survived the night, my husband's chances of survival were 80 percent. That sounded promising to me. We prayed and really thought everything would be okay. Needless to say, other complications developed along with another embolism. This blood clot traveled to his heart and he died. The doctors tried to resuscitate him but to no avail. I recall going in the room where his body laid. He looked peaceful. This gave me a tiny bit of relief because he looked exhausted with the tubes and machines connected to him previously. I asked, "What am I going to do without you?" I truly can say I had no clue. Just like that, I went from being a wife to a widow.

It's amazing what you can remember and what the body holds on to. As I write, details about those days leading up to my husband's death and the days that followed emerge. I can recall the hairstyle I did on the young lady the day before my birthday. I was so excited to leave the salon early that day. I was looking forward to going home, spending time with my family, and cooking dinner. I was eager about my birthday because he always showered me with gifts and surprises. I know it would have been an amazing gift because I later found the cash in his wallet. My husband loved to shop the day of my birthday because I was nosy and checked bank statements online to see where he bought the gifts from.

The body holds on to feelings just like the mind holds memories. My body still feels the uneasiness of when the doctor and chaplain were talking to me. The sensation of the agony overcomes me when I picture giving my cell phone to my mother because I was getting texts wishing me happy birthday. I couldn't bring myself to text them back and let them know I was at the hospital or why.

My heart still breaks when I recall the moment of realizing my husband died. I can *still* sense the tension I felt because I didn't have the strength to call my mother-in-law and tell her that her son died. The lump in my throat forms as I think about the fear I had when informing the children their father died. These are the feelings that stay with you. I didn't find out until much later what to do with those emotions.

Obviously, 2008 was a year of change. I was forced into a lifestyle I didn't sign up for. I could not imagine this in my wildest dream. I had to face a harsh reality and make some tough choices during this time. I was accustomed to being in a partnership and making decisions with my husband. This was no longer an option for me. I was the head of the household now. I had to figure things out quickly. My children depended on me. Just like my mom was strong for me when my uncle died, I thought I had to be strong for them as well.

No one understood what I was going through. No one knew what I was facing. I didn't dare to allow anyone to see the vulnerable side of me. Life was weighing down on me. I was emotionally drained. The emotional turmoil I was going through was unbearable. I would cry myself to sleep at night. Some nights I couldn't sleep because every time I closed my eyes, flashes of my husband would appear. It was months before I could sleep in my own bed. I slept on the sofa for a couple of weeks. Then, I started sleeping in my son's bed. Eventually, I slept in my bed, once I bought a new one. All these little things were happening, and no one knew. I made sure to put on a strong front. If they only knew.

A few months after my husband died, it was confirmed I was pregnant with child number four. This was a shocker. We had tried for two years to conceive another child, but it didn't happen. Now, in the midst of my storm, the rain came down harder. I didn't tell anyone. I was in denial. I only told my friends and family if they asked because there was no denying it once my belly got bigger. My doctor's appointments were the worst. I would go by myself and sit in the car and cry. I'm not sure if I wanted the company. This would mean allowing someone to see me cry. I did my best crying by myself when no one was watching.

In my third trimester of pregnancy, I decided to give my son up for adoption. This was a hard pill to swallow because I had already named him. But, I was not in an emotionally healthy place. I realized children are a gift from God. I thought, why not bestow my gift to another family.

I contacted an adoption agency and started the process. I spent hours looking at family profiles and praying for the right family. I met with one couple and knew right away they were the ones. This was the first major decision I made without my husband and it was a bittersweet moment. I realized I had what's needed to make the decisions necessary to lead this family. I was at peace with my decision. Most did not agree with my choice. Some still look at me funny when I mention it. However, God lead me to do it. My relationship with God kept me grounded and sane during this time. The reality was with the adoption, I suffered another loss. I had learned to suffer in silence.

I read this post by Les Brown a few years later. It stated, "You can start over again! Don't even think about quitting now! It's easy to replay in your mind how things did not work, how much you lost, what you are going through, how angry you are. There is no amount of conversation or magic that is going to wipe the slate clean. You are wasting valuable time and energy that could be used to regain a new normal and start another version of your life. Even though you are hurt and you may be feeling down stop kicking yourself. Face what has happened. Make the decision to start over again.[1]"

That's exactly what I did!

~

DEAR HEAVENLY FATHER,

Transitions are not easy, but I understand they are necessary in order to move forward into our next phase. I pray for serenity and comfort during these difficult times.

In Your Son Jesus Christ Name, Amen

I KNOW, THEY THINK I'M CRAZY!

*"Then I arose in the night, I and a
few men with me; I told no one
what my God had put in my
heart to do at Jerusalem; nor
was there any animal with me,
except the one on which I rode."*
Nehemiah 2:12 NKJV

"Your Grandmother is turning over in her grave!" my aunt protested over the cell phone. She called to lecture me on why I shouldn't let strangers raise my son. My aunt maintained someone in the family should adopt him. She insisted I call the adoption agency and tell them I had a mental breakdown and was depressed after my husband died and made the wrong decision. My aunt pleaded with me to tell them I was under distress when I signed the adoption papers and now I wanted my son back. She used every guilt tactic she could think of to persuade me to change my mind. The phone conversation lasted over an hour. She only decided to end the call because I told her I would think about it.

I was only appeasing her by telling her I would give her demands some thought. The truth is I was adamant with my decision. My mom, dad, and other children didn't voice any objections about the adoption. I'm not sure they didn't say anything because they thought I wouldn't listen because I'm head strong. Nevertheless, I had their support even if they didn't agree with my decision about the adoption. I was firm because I understood and knew this was definitely intended by God. The phone call with my aunt was a few months after my son was born and bonding with his adoptive parents. The decision to gift my son to that couple was not something I took lightly. I prayed constantly before deciding to make that initial call to the adoption agency.

Initially, when my husband died, I was upset with him. I thought he didn't love us enough to fight harder to be with us. I questioned his love for our family. He knew we loved and relied on him. He understood he was my best friend and I could tell him anything and not get judged. He appreciated that the boys looked up to him and he was their role model. We mapped out our 5-year plan. We talked extensively about our future and what we both envisioned for our family. He was finally able to retire from his job and start his own business. He had so much to look forward too. I believed, surely, he wanted to be with us longer and should have fought harder to continue to live on this earth with us.

Eventually, I went from questioning my husband's love for our family to questioning myself. I begin to think I wasn't good enough for him. I thought he was tired of taking care of us. Thoughts of him not wanting to be with me plagued my mind. I was thinking he'd rather die than to be with me. I was mentally attacking myself. I was overwhelmed with guilt, low self-esteem, and depression. I was not in an emotionally healthy place after my husband passed away. I knew I could not raise a newborn under these conditions. I had three other children I couldn't console or comfort because I was stuck in my own grief. God understood my state, in fact, He preordained it. The scripture from Jeremiah 1:5 (NKJV), "Before I formed you in the womb I knew you; before you were born I sanctified you..." comes to mind when I think of that period of my life. I understand in the context of that verse, God was calling Jeremiah to be a prophet. However, that verse also reminds me of God's foresight in our lives.

God allowed me to do something extraordinary even at my lowest point. I must admit, some did not agree with my decision to allow my son to be adopted, such as my aunt who tried desperately to get me to change my mind. Many simply asked why I didn't allow them to adopt my son. I didn't have the answer they wanted to hear. No one understood what I was going through. Therefore, no matter what answer I gave them, it wouldn't suffice. I have learned through this journey, people will question and ask why, but are not always able to handle the answer.

Some of my family members may still wonder

why but don't have the courage to have a conversation with me. Some trusted I made the right decision for my family. I'm not sure of their reasons. I hope this chapter serves as an explanation and offers some comfort and peace as to why. I didn't tell anyone of what God had put in my heart until after I gave birth because I didn't want to compromise on the conviction I was doing God's will. Sometimes when we share with others the details of God's plan for us, they question it because they don't understand. I can accept people asking questions for clarification. However, we don't always have the full picture. We have faith God will see us through it.

God may require you to go against the grain during your grieving process. You should seek wisdom from God before making decisions. Some scholars and therapist suggest waiting a year before making any major changes. That may work for some and for others, God requires swift action. Everyone is not going to understand your rationale. Remember God gave the vision to you. Therefore, others will not see it.

This process is difficult and requires perseverance. Especially if you are a people pleaser. Sometimes, we put things off until it's the right time.

Or, we'll wait because someone told us it's not a good idea. Often, we choose not to do something because we are afraid of stepping on someone's toes. Ask yourself: When is the right time? It's when God calls you to do it. Ask: Who gave you the idea? God planted the seed and now it's time for you to water it and allow it to grow. God will not call you to do something if He hasn't already prepared and made a way for you. Finding your new normal may cause you to lose some friendships. It may require you to get out of your comfort zone. Change is never easy, but it's worth it.

DEAR HEAVENLY FATHER,

Grant me the serenity to accept the things I cannot change, courage to change the things I can, and wisdom to know the difference.[1] *Help me to move forward without condemnation.*

In Your Son Jesus Name, Amen

WHAT AM I GOING TO DO NOW?

"For I know the thoughts that I
think toward you, says
the Lord, thoughts of peace and
not of evil, to give you a future
and a hope. Then you will call
upon Me and go and pray to
Me, and I will listen to
you. And you will seek Me and
find Me, when you search for
Me with all your heart. I will be
found by you, says the Lord,
and I will bring you back from
your captivity; I will gather you
from all the nations and from
all the places where I have

driven you, says the Lord, and I
will bring you to the place from
which I cause you to be carried
away captive."
Jeremiah 29:11-14 NKJV

Questions always seems to linger when grieving. As a matter of fact, questions often plague our thought process. We have so many unanswered questions. Who's going to water the grass? Who's going to greet me when I walk into the house now? What do my friends think of me? Do I cry too much? Do I make others uncomfortable when I walk into a room? Are they inviting me to their party because they feel sorry for me? When should I clean out the closet? Am I going crazy? Are they really concerned for me? Why aren't they checking on me? A ton of questions can race through your mind at any given moment. Sometimes, you just want to scream. And, that's okay. You are allowed to scream.

Grief is not just about someone dying. It's a wide topic that covers a range of losses. I have encountered a number a people that have suffered different types of losses. Divorce, loss of a pet, health diagnosis, getting fired from a job, and incarceration are all forms of loss. People who experience these events process grief as well. They are troubled by the same endless questions. The following stories are a glimpse into what loss resembles in situations besides death. They are based on true events, although the names have been changed.

Jordan was employed at his job for over 15 years. He had plans on retiring in the next five years. He wanted to hit the 20-year mark so he could collect a hefty retirement check. The company had its own retirement board and he would be able to collect a check for him and his wife. Jordan sacrificed holidays, sporting events, and quality time with his family just to meet deadlines. Sometimes, Jordan missed family vacations and important events because the job required him to be there. This job was everything to Jordan; he never thought of leaving or pursuing other career avenues. One day Jordan's boss informed him his management team was fired. One person on the team made a costly mistake and the whole team was fired as a result.

Jordan was devastated. He didn't have anything to do with the other person, so why did he get fired? He was informed he could appeal the decision. He started the appeal process, but it would take a year before his case is heard. The questions stared to come. *How am I going to pay the bills? What other skills do I have? Why me?* Jordan was depressed and snapped at his children for no reason. His wife put off her career transition so that she could make sure the bills were being paid. Jordan's wife was supportive, but that wasn't enough. He was mad at the world and didn't know how to handle being fired. Not only did he lose his job, but he lost his self-worth, self-esteem, and financial security. Jordan's loss was real, and he was experiencing the anger and depression stage of grief at that moment.

Jason adopted Zach 10 years ago. They weathered the storm together. Zach wasn't just a dog, he was Jason's best friend. Zach would sit by the door and wait for Jason to come home. Everyone in the house knew when Jason was close by because Zach would bark and jump with excitement. Jason looked forward to being greeted by Zach. Jason felt Zach was the only one who understood him. Now, he's gone. No one was sure what happened to

Zach. He left the yard one day and did not return. That was so unlike him. The family searched the neighborhood for hours. They emailed pictures to the local animal shelter. They posted ads on social media apps, but no response. Jason checked in the animal shelter for a year. The uncertainty was overwhelming. *Who would take Zach? Did he get hit by a car? Is he still alive? Why did he run away?* Jason's loss was unbearable. He would put off going home because Zach was not there to greet him. Jason was in the denial stage of grief.

Julie worked hard in high school. She maintained the best grades and was awarded for her hard work. She applied to three colleges and was accepted to them all. Julie made the decision to attend college a few hours away from home. Her mom discussed the parties, but she didn't believe it would be like this. There was a party every day of the week. Julie started by going to the parties on the weekends, then eventually she was going during the week. Her grades suffered, and she was kicked out of school. This was an embarrassing time for Julie. She was the first to go to college. Her parents threw her a huge party. Relatives gave her money to go towards her books and living expenses.

Julie didn't understand how her friends were still in college. She failed out and even the community college would not accept her with those grades. Julie's future as she planned it was gone. She dreamed of being a computer engineer—that's a far reach now. Julie's loss of her college plans and career path was devastating. She had no clue of her next steps in life. She only planned on graduating from college. There was no option B with Julie. She cried every night because she knew it was her fault. Julie understood she played a major role in her failing out of college and regretted her decision to let her social life take precedence over her grades. Julie begins to wonder: *What other options do I have? How will I face my family I let down? How can my younger siblings look up to me?* The same questions replayed themselves in her mind. Julie was exhibiting the acceptance and depression stage of grief.

Janice is a single parent of three children. She had plans on traveling the world and be adventurous but decided to wait until the children graduate from high school. She wanted to focus on her children and make sure they were taken care of. Janice advocated for her children and was their biggest supporter. A few years ago, she was sluggish a few days in a row but thought nothing of it. *I'll get some rest this weekend,* Janice thought. One day, she woke up in extreme pain. It was so unbearable that she raced to the emergency room. The doctors couldn't figure out what was going on and sent her home with pain medicine. She had another bout with pain but this time it was sharper, and she couldn't walk. Her sons had to help her to the car. Once again, the doctors could not determine what was causing the pain. Janice decided to call her family doctor to discuss the latest events. Before she could attend her appointment with her family doctor, she was rushed to the emergency room.

This time she was admitted for observations. They ran all types of tests on her. She was in the hospital five days. Janice was diagnosed with lupus. She was in and out of the hospital for over a year. She spent more time in the hospital then her own home. Her health was fading, and the doctors couldn't get the medication to the right dosage. Janice was not accustomed to relying on others for help. She knew her family was willing to support in any capacity they could. She had good days and awful days. Every day, Janice woke up in a different mood. She had plans on traveling. She wanted to be adventurous. All those plans seemed out of reach because of her health concerns. She had to get permission from her doctors just to leave the state. Most days she didn't have the energy to travel. Janice begins to wonder: *Who will take care of my children when I'm in the hospital? Who's going to buy groceries for them? How will I pay my bills? Will my insurance cover these medical costs?* The questions took over Janice's mind and she wasn't able to sleep because of fear and worry. Janice was in the bargaining and depression stage of grief.

Each of the people mentioned suffered some form of loss. They each lost something that was dear to them. All of them had something in common. They were in different stages of grief. They had questions, but no answers.

Eventually, God may supply us with answers. However, we have to accept and trust His will even if those questions remain unanswered.

DEAR HEAVENLY FATHER,

We may never get the answers to our questions. Help us to move forward in spite of.

In Your Son Jesus Name, Amen

JESUS, TAKE THE WHEEL

"Let your gentleness be known to
   all men. The Lord is at hand. Be
   anxious for nothing, but in
   everything by prayer and
   supplication,
   with thanksgiving, let your
   requests be made known to
   God; and the peace of God,
   which surpasses all
   understanding, will guard your
   hearts and minds through
   Christ Jesus."
Philippians 4:5-7 NKJV

My birthday was plagued with sad memories once my husband died. I can tell you I just wanted to do something for me. However, in reality, I really wanted to forget. I wanted to disremember the pain and hurt I was experiencing. I craved a birthday that was normal and void of the emotional turmoil I faced in the past. I was tired of the roller coaster ride. I would go months and things would be great. Then, a scent would cause me to remember or a song on the radio would remind me of my husband.

I accepted my husband was physically gone, still, I was not okay with it. I was not at a point where I could reminisce without feeling sad. I couldn't look at photographs without feeling a wealth of emotions and holding back tears. That was a miserable time for me. I recall a childhood associate asked, "You're not over him, yet?" I didn't respond. I walked away thinking how insensitive that question was. Now, I understand society expects us to continue on with life as usual. As I stated before, I realize some are uncomfortable with people grieving and expressing emotions and expect you to mask your pain and continue as normal.

The expectation of a quick return to normalcy in society is prevalent. Some companies only offer 3-5 days of bereavement. Close friends and family bring food and sit with you for the first few days. However, after the funeral, you are left alone to fend for yourself. No one offers to cook dinner for you and the children a month later because you are expected to be back to normal. Your church family will give you a love offering in a sympathy card within that first week. But what happens the following week? Someone might ask you, "How are you doing?" Often, the grieving is left to their own devices soon after the funeral. I understand the world continues to move, nonetheless, some need time to process what happened and adjust. Some just need a shoulder to cry on every now and then. Healing is a process that requires time and patience.

I was trying to move forward and continue as if nothing had changed as expected by society. I tried to behave normal. I held back tears because I didn't want others to look at me differently. I put on a strong front because that's what I thought was anticipated from others. I soon realized my life would never be the same. It was useless trying to navigate life as if my husband was still alive. The truth is, I was running around like a chicken with its head cut off. I was sleep deprived, frustrated, and tired. I had to create a new normal for myself and my children. This meant changes were on the horizon. I had to scale back and not allow the children to participate in as many activities. I was one person trying to fill the shoes of two. It was not working, and changes had to take place.

I learned at an early age when we encounter loss that we should go on with life as if nothing happened. After my uncle died, I don't recall any major changes. Everyone continued to move forward. When we encounter an obstacle or traumatic events, changes are inevitable. I learned in this process life will continue to change and we must embrace the changes as we discover what our new normal is.

I'm not saying it will be easy to move forward. In fact, if I can be transparent with you, it will be difficult because as humans we cling to familiar things. We like having things in a certain order and being habitual. New can be challenging for some. Change is definitely not a smooth transition for all.

I had to recognize that I needed to alter some things before a transformation could take place.

I had to accept I was a single parent and what I did affected my children as well as me. I had to recognize I didn't have all the answers and be comfortable with not knowing. My prayer life and relationship with God grew immensely. I talked to God about everything. This was new territory for me and I needed to seek God's counsel and guidance. I truly believe if we trust God, He will direct our paths.

DEAR HEAVENLY FATHER,

Thank You for guiding us this far. Thank You for the journey even though we might have chosen a different path. Thank You for moving us forward in the direction we needed to go.

In Your Son Jesus Name, Amen

THE ROLLERCOASTER

"Blessed are those who mourn, For
they shall be comforted."
Matthew 5:4 NKJV

"Yea, though I walk through the
valley of the shadow of death, I
will fear no evil; For
You are with me; Your rod and
Your staff, they comfort me."
Psalm 23:4 NKJV

Eight months after my husband died I moved to another state to be closer to family. My sons grew up without really knowing our extended family and I thought they would benefit being around them. Also, this was the fresh start we needed. I managed to enroll myself in college. I started working in a salon and gaining new clientele. I was beginning to see the light.

My sons were doing well in school. They were 13 and 9 years old and my daughter was only 2 years old when my husband died. It was a rough start for us initially; however, we were able to adjust after a while. My sons were playing sports and joining different organizations. We joined a new church and begin to meet new friends and associates. We all appeared to adjust to this new life. I didn't have the word 'widow' stamped on my forehead. No one knew I was a widow unless I revealed it to them and that was seldom. If anyone asked if I was married, I would simply say no without any explanation. People knew me as a single mother with three children. I thought everything was going well. I

Two years passed and decided to throw myself a

birthday party to celebrate this newfound happiness. I wanted to observe my birthday with family and friends I recently met. I was so excited. I was happy and beginning to enjoy life again. I wasn't crying anymore. I was spending time with family and loving every minute of it. I was socializing again and living life. It appeared to most I was back to normal. The planning and preparing for my birthday celebration was fun and exciting. I was able to focus on something other than my children and school. It had been a few years since I hosted an event and invited people other than family. The celebration was a success. Everyone who was invited came out to help me celebrate. Even old classmates I'd reconnected with joined the celebration. This was the most fun I'd had in a long time.

The next morning, I woke up and walked into my bathroom. I immediately dropped to the floor and wailed like never before. I couldn't tell you what bought this sudden sadness on. I cannot explain what overcame me. The day before, I was happy and celebrating my birthday. Now, I'm sitting on my bathroom floor crying and feeling as though I was back in the hospital when I got the news my husband coded. The memories of that night were so vivid at that moment, I forgot momentarily that it had happened two years ago. I'm not sure how long I stayed on that floor. But I remember thinking, *I thought the worst part was over*.

That's the thing with grief. You simply do not get over it, you take one day at a time. We strive to live another day without our love one. In some cases, we learn to live another day without that job we valued or another day not in our best health that we took for granted. It gets easier overtime for some. Others may require more healing. Everyone is unique, and every relationship is irreplaceable.

There is no simple way to describe grief. It's an unexplainable deep sorrow. There's not one single definition that completely embraces the word. There are several attempts to explain what grief is. However, it is impossible to find a working definition that fits everyone and all situations. Elisabeth Kübler-Ross is a psychiatrist and author. She is widely known for her explanation of the pattern of adjustment after grief. Kübler-Ross explained the five stages of grief are denial, anger, bargaining, depression, and acceptance.[1] These stages are not in any particular sequence. The stages of grief are not linear. Some experience all five stages and others only experience two or three. There is no timeframe for one to experience these stages.

These are explanation of how some navigate and adjust after experiencing a loss.

Denial is one of the first stages of grief for most. Some have an overwhelming feeling of shock and numbness. It's hard to accept or imagine life without what we lost. Those survival questions begin to consume us. We wonder if or how we can continue. Anger is another stage of the grieving process. It involves pain. We are angry because we're in pain. As humans, pain is an unwanted feeling. Therefore, we tend to express it in unhealthy ways. We may become angry at God or the person that dies. Some are furious at themselves for not doing more. These are normal emotions and feelings. As stated previously, I was angry at my deceased husband for months. Eventually, I blamed myself for not doing more and thinking I was not good enough for him to fight to stay alive.

Depression is a familiar feeling for some because it is necessary in the grieving process. The emptiness sets in and we think it will not get better. It presents itself in a number of ways. Some have trouble eating, sleeping, getting out of bed, and carrying out daily routines. Some people learn to mask the depression because it can be seen as unhealthy. Depression after losing a loved one is natural. It's not something you can wave a magic wand to get rid of. It is important to remember not to let the grief consume you. There is hope and light at the end of the tunnel.

Bargaining and acceptance are the other stages of grief discussed by Kübler-Ross. The terms are self-explanatory. Some try to bargain and question God. We want to negotiate more time or not feeling the way we do. Acceptance is a difficult stage. I believe it's tough because we have to accept the finality of the physical being of our love one. Acceptance represents the conclusiveness of the job we dedicated our life to, or compliant that a marriage is over. Some things are hard to accept. Who wants to recognize a marriage after 35 years is over? This stage does not mean we are okay with our situation. It simply means we accept life will not be the same. We have to continue on and find a new normal.

My experience with grief has been like a roller-coaster ride. I understand there will be some up and downs, sudden jerks, and an upside-down experience, but I never know when to expect it. I have come to learn some can ride the exact same rollercoaster and leave with two different experiences. Some ride the same rollers coaster twice, but the turns still surprise them. All rollercoasters have the same premise. A series of drastic changes without warning. Some have steep drops, tight turns, and you can find them anywhere. Keep in mind rollercoasters restrain you. Even if you want to get off, it's impossible until the end of the ride.

DEAR HEAVENLY FATHER,

Loss is something we cannot avoid and must all endure. I pray You wrap your loving arms around us and grant us the comfort needed to move forward one day at a time. Help us maneuver this grieving process and remember we are not alone on this journey. Help us to recollect You are with us every step of the way. I pray we seek answers from You and understand nothing happens to us, but for us.

In Your Son Jesus Name. Amen

PEOPLE SAY THE CRAZIEST
THINGS

"The Spirit of the Lord God is upon
Me Because the Lord has
anointed Me To preach good
tidings to the poor; He has sent
Me to heal the brokenhearted,"
Isaiah 61:1 NKJV

"God is in the midst of her, she
shall not be moved; God shall
help her, just at the break of
dawn."
Psalm 46:5 NKJV

Years ago, my friend's mother passed away. She decided not to have a wake or funeral at her mother's request. My friend's mother knew she was dying and explained she wanted friends and family to remember her the way she was prior to being diagnosed with cancer. She asked to be cremated and shared her reasoning with my friend. This was a tough task for my friend to carry out. In the end, she honored her mother's wishes and decided to have a memorial instead. Friends and family were allowed to pay their final respect and view the body at the funeral home.

A group of us decided to go to the funeral home at the same time. We wanted to comfort and support our friend. I recall standing in line to view the body. My friend was standing there next to her mom's coffin. She greeted everyone who came to pay their respects. She had this look of despair on her face. I knew how difficult this must have been for her. She was sobbing and still managed to hug and thank everyone who supported her. I thought how painful it must be to stand beside your mother's open coffin and greet everyone.

There were only a few people in front of me

before I had a chance to view the body and greet my friend. I continued to witness her interactions with others. I heard an older woman in front of me tell my friend, "Be strong for your mom," as she hugged her.

I politely waited my turn to greet and hug my friend. The words from the older woman were still lingering in my mind. I never thought about what I was going to say to my friend. I was lost in thought about things I was witnessing while standing in line. It was now my turn. I looked at her mom laying peacefully in her coffin. I looked at my friend and just hugged her. The words flowed. I told her she did not have to be strong for anyone. I expressed she didn't have to stand beside her mom's coffin and greet everyone. I voiced to her she was free to cry as much as she needed to because this was hard.

I knew first-hand how it felt to lose a loved one. The phrase, "be strong" caused something in me to want to protect my friend. It also stirred emotions in me. I didn't know the person who told her that, but I was angry at her. I was upset because I thought that's the last thing my friend needs to hear standing next to her deceased mother. How strong can anyone be standing for hours and greeting friends, family, and strangers? How strong do you have to be to realize these people are coming here to say good-bye to your mother? I was upset because many had whispered, "be strong" to me as well.

In fact, I have come to understand the phrase, "be strong" are not words of comfort. I recognize people tell us this out of love because either they've heard someone else say it or it was said to them in their time of grief. However, I do not think people grasp the implications of the term "be strong." It is not explicitly stated, but it's understood as "do not cry in front of me."

The words "be strong" are an unrealistic demand placed on grieving people. I realize some are not comfortable with emotions. Therefore, they tell the grieving person to be strong simply because they are not strong enough to handle you expressing feelings.

In another incident, a relative's dad died. My relative is in her early 30s. She helped her mom take care of her father for over three years before he passed away. She was devastated because she realized her father will not walk her down the aisle for her wedding and her children will never meet and know their grandfather.

I attended the funeral. My relative could not sit through all of it and walked out of the church. I followed her because I was concerned. Another relative saw her as well. We both stayed with her outside.

I understood the power of silence and let her cry. The other relative stated, "It will be okay, and it will get better." She was absolutely right. Life will be better one day at a time and she will learn to live on without her dad. However, those were not the words she needed to hear at that very moment. She needed time to cry. It hurts like hell to have to bury someone you love. The moment you look at their coffin and realize that person is physically gone is extremely difficult. Someone telling you it will get better is not a consolation prize and does not make you feel any better.

I understand some do not know what to say when in the presence of a grieving person. People try to offer words of comfort. I find people in uncomfortable circumstances often say things that do not make logical sense. Grief is very uncomfortable; therefore, it is reasonable for people to say illogical things. Sometimes, the best thing to say is nothing. They may only need you to be there at that moment. Some just need a friend or relative to hold their hand while crying. The best words can be unspoken.

I recall while I was planning the funeral for my husband. I kept busy. I didn't have time to think about life afterwards because I was in the midst of making sure the final arrangements were taking care of. Visitors constantly came to bring food or check in on me during that first week. My best friend requested time off from work to be with me during the planning process. However, it was after the funeral that I needed people the most.

The best timing for support can be after the funeral. Friends and family go back to their normal lives. The grieving person is left to figure out how to go on. They may be struggling with getting out of the bed or deciding how to maneuver through the day. This is the time a grief-stricken person is most vulnerable because everyone else has moved on and they are trying to reconcile a life without the person who died.

DEAR HEAVENLY FATHER,

Thank You for helping and guiding us to move forward one day at a time. I understand we may not always know what to say. Give us the words to heal and not destroy. I ask that You use us as vessel to help others. Our tragedy can also be our testimony. Please ease our minds and hearts with peace.

In Your Son Jesus Name, Amen

HELP!

"Ask, and it will be given to you;
seek, and you will find; knock,
and it will be opened to you.
For everyone who asks receives,
and he who seeks finds, and to
him who knocks it will be
opened."
Matthew 7:7-8 NKJV

A month after my husband died, my uncle came to visit the children and me. His wife had passed away a year earlier and he wanted to offer some advice. He bought some material about a support group he joined. My uncle explained that African Americans often do not know how to grieve, and he suggested I sit in with the support group at least once. He explained the group helped him process his thoughts and feelings. My uncle felt the support group could do the same for me.

My uncle was not the person who gives out advice. Therefore, I considered the things he told me. I didn't take it lightly because I knew he cared for the kids and my well-being. My uncle only wanted to see me heal. I didn't know he'd joined a support group after his wife's death. Obviously, it helped him because he was now passing the information on to me. I realize he was right about me not knowing how to grieve. As I explained previously, I tried to move forward as if my life did not drastically change. I appeared fine on the outside, but I was really falling apart. Therefore, I decided to give the group a chance.

The support group was a 12-week program and it was already underway. The group met every week and was in week three. My uncle accompanied me to the first meeting. I didn't know what to expect. I was anxious walking in through the doors. I was relieved my uncle was with me because all the attention would not be directed towards me. The facilitator introduced us and offered her story on how she became the facilitator. Next, my uncle shared his testimony on how the group helped him. The facilitator asked if I wanted to share anything, but I declined. Others in the group shared their stories as well. I left feeling relieved. Even though I didn't say anything, it was a relief to be among others who shared the same pain I did.

Joining the support group was what I needed at the time. Eventually, I opened up and shared my experience. For the first time, I realized I wasn't going crazy. I understood the rollercoaster of emotions were normal. It felt great sharing with others who experienced similar losses. Also, the group allowed me to be me. I didn't have to hold back tears or say I was fine when in actuality I was falling apart. I felt normal being amongst the members. Listening to others allowed me to take my mind off my loss for a moment and feel sympathy for others. The support group helped me through some tough times.

In 2013, I sought the help of a therapist. I realized there were some unresolved issues I needed to work through. The therapist helped me as well, but in a different manner. The support group provided me with normalcy. The therapist was one-on-one and permitted me the opportunity to come to my own resolutions. I came to realize I was still holding on to some anger and resentment. I was still upset my husband died. I loved and missed him dearly; however, I was holding on to what used to be. I had to let go of the past and look forward to the future. Letting go of the past didn't mean forgetting my husband, it simply meant allowing myself to create a new life and redefining myself in the process.

In both instances, I did what was best for me at that particular time in my life. I understand everyone is not comfortable with talking to others. However, sometimes you have to step outside of your comfort zone for healing and clarity. No matter what your loss is—a job, divorce, health, or a loved one—you should seek help. Remember, grief is like a rollercoaster ride. It's filled with ups and downs. Occasionally, when you're down, it can take you to a place that's hard to come back from. Talking to others who understand and can relate to you is helpful.

It is helpful to know yourself. Initially, I joined a support group. That may not be what's needed for you. Some require one-on-one after those first months of the loss. While others may need to listen to others to take their mind off their grief. It is important to know limits and what you are comfortable with so that you can make the best choice for you.

Keep in mind, it's okay to change your mind. You may think you need a group, but after two meetings you realize a therapist might be best. Do not allow yourself to be somewhere that is not helping you heal. Be open-minded and committed to the process and understand it requires work on your part as well. The support group and therapist can only do so much for you.

As you can see, I did not do it by myself. I had to seek the help of others. Don't be afraid to reach out for help. First, I joined a support group. Years later, I sought a therapist. Healing takes time and you might find yourself needing a refresher years later. It's never too late to ask for help. There are many options available to those needing help. Many churches are now offering counseling free of charge. Some have professional licensed counselors on staff. The internet is a great resource for finding support groups. Call and ask questions to make sure it's the right fit for you. Take the first step in your healing.

Each person's loss is different. It's not just you that is affected by it. Your spouse and children are affected as well. They may require help, also. Keep in mind everyone's reaction to the loss is unique and therefore they should attend a separate group or counselor than you. Each family member is affected in a different manner and requires their own space initially. Everyone can come together after the healing process has begun.

DEAR HEAVENLY FATHER,

I pray You remove the fear of asking for help from anyone reading this book. I understand pride and appearance can hold us back. I ask that You release the bondage that's holding us back from seeking what's needed for our healing. Thank You for moving us forward in the restoration process.

In Your Son Jesus Name, Amen

A MESSAGE FROM ABOVE

*"Not that I have already attained,
or am already perfected; but I
press on, that I may lay hold of
that for which Christ Jesus has
also laid hold of me. Brethren, I
do not count myself to have
apprehended; but one thing I
do, forgetting those things
which are behind and reaching
forward to those things which
are ahead, I press toward the
goal for the prize of the upward
call of God in Christ Jesus."
Philippians 3:12-14 NKLV*

My husband and I meet at a pop-up book store. I was working as a temporary employee at his place of employment. I was only scheduled to work there a few days. I recall arriving at work and the young lady in charge informed me there was a pop-up book store on the first floor. I settled in and headed downstairs to see if there was anything I was interested in. My uncle who resided in Louisiana asked me several times to mail him books to read to pass time. I figured this would be my opportunity to buy him a few books. I was standing there reading the back cover of a T.D. Jakes book. I was trying to figure out which books to send my uncle.

I heard this strong yet gentle voice say nervously, "Good morning." I didn't think anyone was speaking to me, so I kept on reading and never looked up. When I turned around, I almost bumped into him. He asked my name and if I would call him sometime. I informed him of my name, wrote down his number, but didn't have any intentions on calling him. Initially, I thought he was nervous speaking to me, then it dawned on me he had a speech impediment—he stuttered. I must admit, I judged him because he stuttered. I thought it would never work because I would not understand anything he said.

A few weeks later, I was assigned to his place of employment again. I was sitting at a table eating lunch by myself. He came and sat down at the table. Of course, he asked why I didn't call. I told him I was busy. That didn't stop him from continuing on with the conversation. It wasn't as bad as I thought. We got married a few months later. I asked why he decided to ask me on a date. He said it was because when he walked in the bookstore, I had a halo above my head like an angel. I thought, *Yeah right*. He always stuck to his story when asked.

In 2013, I was driving my son back to college. It was a three-hour drive and I think he fell asleep halfway through the ride. I started reminiscing about my husband and how proud he would've been to see him in college. Then, I thought about all the times I could have been more supportive of my husband when he was alive. He was always coming up with various ideas on what type of business to start. I started talking to my husband and asking for forgiveness. I told him I should have been more supportive. All this took place while I was driving. By the time we exited for my son's school, my eyes were red due to me crying.

I wanted to fill my car with gas before driving back home. I asked my son to pump the gas. Usually, I'd sit in the car while he does this. However, I wanted to put some water on my face and get something to drink. I walked in and noticed the cashier looking at me. He looked as if he was about 20 years old. I proceeded to the restroom and afterwards picked a soda from the cooler. As I walked to the cash register, the cashier was now staring at me. I put my drink on the counter. The cashier blushed and asked me to forgive him for staring. I told him no worries and continued to pay for my items. The young man gave me my change and explained he was staring because it appeared as if I had a halo like an angel above my head. It took everything in me not to scream, but I knew at that moment things would be fine.

I realized I was harboring feelings of guilt without knowing it. I didn't realize this could have potentially been holding me back from finding my new normal. That night, God knew what I needed to hear. He delivered the message through a complete stranger. But, I heard it loud and clear.

I was not expecting the cashier to say the same thing my deceased husband told me years before. Some may say it was a coincidence. I certainly do not believe I'm an angel. However, whatever the case, I got what was needed to move forward and stop feeling guilty. Yes, I do believe I could have done some things differently. I forgive myself. I freed myself from feelings of guilt. This was only the beginning.

In times of grief, most people may experience feelings of guilt after a loss. This is not what God intends for us. God wants us to grieve our loss, but not continue to worry about what we did wrong. We often think of what could have been said or done. Some blame themselves for not being there. Others wish they could have spent more time with the person before they died. We think about what we could have done to prevent them from dying.

Even divorcees think about what they could have done to prevent the divorce from occurring. Some blame themselves for getting fired from their job. Sometimes, it's God moving you in a different direction and He knew you wouldn't do it on your own. Some of the issues we face every day are no one's fault. It's insane and silly for us to blame ourselves for the losses we experience. We should continue to praise God for the time and experience and ask for healing from it.

I understand all these thoughts go through your mind. Try not to focus on what could have been and redirect your attention on what is. It's okay to wish things could have been handled differently. This is how we learn from our past. We apply the knowledge gained to our future.

After the incident with the cashier, I knew I was moving in the right direction. I noticed right away, on the ride back home, I was at peace with myself. Releasing guilt is a must in the healing process. God used a complete stranger for me, but He may use other tools to help you. Be open and remember, nothing happens by coincidence but by divine providence. I didn't go out searching to relieve this guilt nor was I even aware that I was harboring it. At that moment God moved my grief to grace.

Dear Heavenly Father,

I pray the person reading this book is free from the feel-

ings of guilt. Help them to understand loss is part of life and we can never be prepared. But we can be healed. Help them to move forward beyond the grief to begin a new day.

In Your Son Jesus Name, Amen

WHO AM I, AND HOW DID I GET HERE?

"What profit has the worker from that in which he labors? I have seen the God-given task with which the sons of men are to be occupied. He has made everything beautiful in its time. Also He has put eternity in their hearts, except that no one can find out the work that God does from beginning to end. I know that nothing is better for them than to rejoice, and to do good in their lives, and also that every man should eat and

drink and enjoy the good of all
his labor—itisthe gift of God."
Ecclesiastes 3:9-13 NKJV

Who am I, and how did I get here? These questions are ones I often ask myself. They are simple, but yet complex. This journey has taught me I am constantly evolving and changing. The person I was five years or ten years ago is not the person I am today. I am not the same person prior to writing this book. Some attributes about me will always be the same. I will always be a Christian, African American female.

I cannot change that. I didn't wake up and notice a different me. This is a gradual process, and I am a willing participant. I embrace change now because I know it's part of finding my new normal.

Merriam-Webster defines normal as, "conforming to a type, standard, or regular pattern," or "of, relating to, or characterized by average intelligence or development." It is impossible to continue the same pattern after a loss. I understand we have been programmed to think a return to normalcy is expected. How can you continue to live as nothing happened when a part of you is missing? You cannot. You must find a new way of doing things. You have to find your new normal. Do not allow society to dictate who you are. We are not settlers, we are survivors.

I know humans are not average because Genesis 1:26 informs us, *Then God said, "Let Us make man in Our image, according to Our likeness; let them have dominion over the fish of the sea, over the birds of the air, and over the cattle, overall the earth and over every creeping thing that creeps on the earth."* We are uniquely made in the image of God. There is nothing typical about us. God does not intend for us to settle for average. He wants us to continue to strive for more. That's why He is always planting new ideas in us. He will not allow us to rest until His will is carried out.

Finding my new normal was a process. I had to figure out what was stopping me from moving forward. I had to release the pain of being a widow. I had to push past what I thought was expected of me. I realized everyone have adversities in life. How we handle those incidents dictates our future. I had to process my situation and determine the best route for me and my children. I could not live by someone else's rules.

Once again, I cannot emphasize the importance of seeking help. I had to talk to someone. I sought professional help. This helped me move past a phase I was stuck in. I understood that I didn't have all the answers and was comfortable with not knowing. I knew eventually God would give me the tools needed to move forward.

I had to redefine myself. I was so caught up in being a wife and mother, I did not have my own identity outside of those two roles. Sometimes, we invest all of our time and energy on others and neglect ourselves.

Now, I choose to put myself first. This meant telling others no and letting some people down. I had to get to know myself. The best thing you can do for yourself is to allow yourself some "me" time.

I went on lunch dates by myself. I enjoyed going to the movies and other events alone. I still love my alone time. It allows me to think, map out my future, and keep the focus on myself. I figured out what I liked and didn't like. I identified my values. I sought after what was important to me.

I set goals I wanted to achieve. I visualized

what I wanted and went after it. I went back to school and earned my bachelor's degree. I wanted to be a teacher. I graduated with a minor in education. However, I realized God was calling me to do other things as well.

So, I went back to school again to continue my education and earned my master's degree in another field. It's okay to change your mind and decide to take another route. Remember, we are on a journey. We are moving from one phase of our life to another. Sometimes, there will be a road block and other times a fork in the road. You can take whichever road that leads to your destination. But realize, the paths will be different and embrace that difference. I committed to the process of going to school, I was determined to finish. I remained focused and stayed on the path that was laid out for me.

Earlier in this book, I mentioned feelings of frustration and anger. I channeled those feelings into something productive. I went to the gym and worked out during my breaks at school. I parked at the far end of school, so I would have to walk a long stretch to class.

It's easy to lash out at others when we are upset. It's hard to focus that energy on something positive. Working out may not be for you, but there are other things you can do. Writing, painting, bicycling, walking, or kick boxing are ways to let go of some of that frustration. Find whatever you like, be open, and commit to the process.

Don't let this world make you think you are stuck; move forward with purpose. If you find yourself in doubt, think of the words of Former First Lady Michelle Obama, "When you are struggling, and you start thinking about giving up, I want you to remember something that my husband and I have talked about since we first started this journey nearly a decade ago—something that has carried us through every moment in this White House and every moment of our lives—and that is the power of hope. The belief that something better is always possible if you're willing to work for it and fight for it."[1] We all have a purpose and God has laid the foundation for us to fulfill it.

This journey has taught me a great deal about myself. Once again, the questions: "Who am I, and how did I get here?" are consistently being redefined. I am intentional about my actions and decisions. I am persistent, courageous, and a fighter. I am willing to explore new opportunities and embrace challenges. I am here because God trusts me with His plans. I am unapologetic.

We serve an awesome God and He can turn your tragedy into your testimony. He will redefine you in the midst of your turmoil. I am constantly redefining myself and creating my new normal. Today, my tragedy is my testimony and this is my story about how, just like that, I went from being a wife to a widow and my glorious journey of growing from grief to grace.

DEAR HEAVENLY FATHER,

Thank You for the opportunity to bear witness to Your awesomeness. Thank You for guidance. I pray whomever reads this book is restored and replenished. Continue to use me as a vessel as I move forward with Your will for me.

In Your Son Jesus Name, Amen

"You will keep him in perfect
   peace,
Whose mind is stayed on You,
Because he trusts in You.
Isaiah 26:3 NKJV

Writing this book has been a great experience. I've rehashed some memories that I'd forgotten and reminisced on some fun and not so terrific times. I wouldn't trade this experience.

The journey of accomplishing the writing of this book reminds me of the time I went zip-lining for the first time. It was an interesting experience to say the least. I was on vacation with my best friend and wanted to try something new. This experience would also help me conquer my fear of heights. The idea of zip-lining was completely my idea and I think my friend just went along. We made it to the sight and started putting on the gear. My nerves were starting to get the best of me. I went to the restroom at least twice before the guide lead us to the course.

The guide explained there were six zip-lines we had to cross before getting the main line that was 49 yards (147 feet) above ground and through the jungle. We had to climb a tree to get to the first zip-line. The climb was longer and scarier than the actual zip-line. My heart was racing, and I was thinking, *Why did I signed up for this?* The guide connected me to the harness. My hands were sweating, and I was nervous. I felt my stomach drop as soon as he asked if I was ready. I said, "Yes!" even though I wasn't. My eyes were shut tight and I could feel myself moving fast. I finally got the courage to open my eyes. The scenery was beautiful and mind blowing. I couldn't believe I was zip-lining through a jungle in Mexico!

The scene from the top was amazing. It appeared like I was flying through trees.

The first two zip-lines were short and prepared newcomers for what lies ahead. The rest of the zip-lines were needed to reach our final destination. During the final stretch through the jungle, the guide informed us we would be upside down like Spiderman in the movies. Leading up to this point, I was comfortable but didn't think I was ready to be upside down. Once it was my turn, I decided to go for it. The rush that overcame me was like no other. I laughed and smiled the entire time flying through the jungle. I did not have any regrets.

Just like my experience with zip-lining, I was nervous and excited about writing this book. God gave me the vision to do this; however, when I decided to follow the call I had anxiety and wanted to turn around. The lead-up to writing the book was worse than actually writing the book.

I sat down to write the Introduction and the first chapter. They were short and prepared me for what laid ahead. The chapters in the middle, like zip-lining, were essential in getting to the finale. Chapter 10 served as a release and a rush. When it was over, I thought, *It's not so bad. I would definitely do it again.*

This journey has taught me a valuable lesson. God will not call you to something He did not prepare you to do. God gave me the vision and He ushered me through the process. I had no idea what I would include in this book. I knew my testimony would help some going through a tough time dealing with loss. It has been a pleasure to share my experience with you. Thank you for taking the time to read my book, and I pray it helps you on your journey to finding your new normal.

Today my new normal is being a great mother to three beautiful children, finding love again, and being an awesome wife to my new husband. I am a licensed LPC. I am a student continuing my education to pursue my PhD. I am the founder and director of a nonprofit organization that mentors teenagers and young women. I help women set goals and keep them accountable. And now, I am an author…

Dear Heavenly Father,

Thank You for using me as a vessel to help others that are traveling the same path. Thank You for trusting me to carry out Your plans. Thank You for the shift and break-through. And thank You, thank You, thank You for helping me find my new normal.

In Your Son Jesus Name, Amen

ABOUT THE AUTHOR

Shannon Davis-Wills is a native of New Orleans, Louisiana; today she resides in Texas. She is a wife and a mother of three amazing children. Shannon is the founder and director of the non-profit organization, *Moving Forward with Purpose*. Their mission is to provide girls and women with the courage/guidance needed to redefine themselves and achieve personal goals. Shannon is committed to empowering women with the confidence to push through the adversities of life as they discover their new normal.

Shannon believes every woman has the ability to redirect her path to fulfill her God given purpose. Shannon's life experiences and education qualifies her to be an excellent source of inspiration. Her message *Finding One's New Normal* is moving, inspiring, powerful and motivating as women discover their new normal.

Shannon holds a Bachelor's Degree in Humanities and a Master's Degree in Professional Counseling.

I want to take this time to thank you for reading my journey about growing from grief to grace. I would love to receive your feedback and hear from you. Please feel free to contact me via email: shannon@movingforwardwithpurpose.com

You may also post comments on my author page: www.findingyournewnormal.org

I am available for interviews, speaking engagements, and other publicity matters. Please feel free to email me at: shannon@movingforwardwithpurpose.com

Lastly, will you do me a favor? Please go online and leave a book review from wherever you purchased my book. Thanks for your support!

REFERENCE PAGE

2. HOW TO CRY WHEN NO ONE IS LOOKING

1. Les, Brown. Facebook, 8 October 2014, 11:02 p.m., https://www.facebook.com/thelesbrown/posts. Accessed 27 October 2018.

3. I KNOW, THEY THINK I'M CRAZY!

1. Niebuhr, Reinhold. Serenity Prayer. 1951., Accessed 6 January 2019. Retrieved from http://www.sandersweb.net/ed/OriginalSerenityPrayer.html

6. THE ROLLERCOASTER

1. Elisabeth Kübler-Ross Biography. ERKFoundation. 2018., https://www.ekrfoundation.org/elisabeth-kubler-ross/ Assessed 25 November 2018.

10. WHO AM I, AND HOW DID I GET HERE?

1. Gonzales, Erica. The 10 Most Inspiring Quotes from Michelle Obama's Final Speech as First Lady. Harper's Bazaar. Accessed 30 December 2018 Retrieved from https://www.harpersbazaar.com/culture/features/news/a19783/michelle-obama-final-speech-best-quotes/

Made in the USA
Columbia, SC
27 March 2019